WORLD CUP

ALL-TIME GREATS

BY ANTHONY STREETER

Book design by Jake Slavik
Cover design by Jake Slavik

Photographs ©: Maxime Le Pihif/Sipa/AP Images, cover (top), 1 (top); AP Images, cover (bottom), 1 (bottom); 4Imagens/Hulton Archive/Getty Images, 4; Central Press/Hulton Archive/Getty Images, 7; Paul Bereswill/Getty Images Sport/Getty Images, 9; Shaun Botterill/Getty Images Sport/Getty Images, 10; Laurence Griffiths/Getty Images Sport/Getty Images, 12; Catherine Ivill/Getty Images Sport/Getty Images, 14; Rick Stewart/Allsport/Getty Images Sport/Getty Images, 16; Minas Panagiotakis/Getty Images Sport/Getty Images, 19; Kevin C. Cox/Getty Images Sport/Getty Images, 20

Press Box Books, an imprint of Press Room Editions.

ISBN
978-1-63494-867-8 (library bound)
978-1-63494-885-2 (paperback)
978-1-63494-920-0 (epub)
978-1-63494-903-3 (hosted ebook)

Library of Congress Control Number: 2024901034

Distributed by North Star Editions, Inc.
2297 Waters Drive
Mendota Heights, MN 55120
www.northstareditions.com

Printed in the United States of America
082024

ABOUT THE AUTHOR

Anthony Streeter is a former sportswriter who has written for various newspapers. He lives in Columbia, Missouri, with his wife and three kids.

TABLE OF CONTENTS

PELÉ
10

CHAPTER 1

STARS OF THE WORLD

Modern soccer started in England in the 1800s. By the early 1900s, the game was spreading around the world. Top men's national teams began playing in the Olympic Games. Team captain **José Nasazzi** helped Uruguay win the 1924 and 1928 Olympic gold medals. In 1930, Uruguay hosted the first World Cup. Nasazzi led his country to the title.

Brazil arrived at the 1958 World Cup with a secret weapon. **Pelé**, a 17-year-old forward, scored six goals. Two came in the final against Sweden as Brazil won its first championship.

Pelé went on to play in three more World Cups. Brazil won two of them. Pelé did more than just score. His movements and ball control left defenders feeling helpless.

Brazil ran through its opponents on the way to the final in 1970. Team captain **Carlos Alberto** played shutdown defense at right back. In the final, he scored a famous goal. Almost every Brazil player touched the ball in the build-up. Many consider this Brazil squad to be soccer's best team ever.

England hosted the 1966 World Cup. The home team made a run to the final. There, forward **Geoff Hurst** scored three goals.

STAT SPOTLIGHT

WORLD CUP RECORD

YOUNGEST GOAL SCORER

Pelé: 17 years, 239 days (June 19, 1958)

He became the first player to score a hat trick in a World Cup final. Those goals helped England secure its lone World Cup title.

Center back **Franz Beckenbauer** lost in the 1966 final. But the West German grew into a great leader. In 1974, Beckenbauer's playmaking ability from the back propelled his country to the championship.

The 1986 World Cup is best remembered for **Diego Maradona**. The Argentine attacker stunned the world in the quarterfinals. First, he scored a goal that appeared to go in off his hand. The referee didn't see it, so the goal counted. Four minutes later, Maradona got the ball 70 yards from goal. Then he dribbled past five English defenders to score again. It's one of the most famous goals of all time. Maradona ended the tournament with five goals as Argentina beat West Germany to win the title.

JUST GREAT

Just Fontaine dominated the 1958 World Cup. In six games, the little-known French forward scored 13 goals. That's still the record for the most goals in a single tournament. Three others eventually scored more in their careers. However, each played in at least twice as many games as Fontaine.

Argentina and West Germany met again in the 1990 World Cup final. This time West Germany won. Beckenbauer coached the team.

But midfielder **Lothar Matthäus** captained the West Germans to a 1–0 win. He went on to play in a fifth World Cup in 1998. Matthäus became the first non-goalie to play in that many tournaments.

ZIDANE
10

CHAPTER 2

GLOBAL GAME-CHANGERS

France's team at the 1998 World Cup was described as a rainbow. Its players came from many ethnic groups. **Zinedine Zidane** shined brightest. The midfielder controlled games with his playmaking skills. In the final, he scored twice and led France to its first championship. Zidane led his team back to the final in 2006. But he received a red card in the game, and France went on to lose.

Many fans had expected Brazilian striker **Ronaldo** to be the star of the 1998 World

Cup final. However, Brazil fell to France that year. In 2002, though, Ronaldo and the Brazilians were unstoppable. Ronaldo scored a tournament-leading eight goals. Two came in the final as Brazil beat Germany 2–0. The win gave Brazil a record fifth championship.

Italy claimed its fourth championship in 2006. **Gianluigi Buffon** was a big reason why. The goalie gave up only two goals in seven matches. One was an own goal. The other came on a penalty kick. Buffon eventually played in 14 games across four World Cups.

Spain's 2010 team didn't have an individual player who dominated. Instead, the players overwhelmed opponents by working together. Spain's talented midfielders all played an essential role. But **Andrés Iniesta** became the hero. His goal in extra time clinched Spain's first championship.

A new teenage star emerged in 2018. The speedy **Kylian Mbappé** burst up and down the wing for France. He had scored three goals before

GERMAN STRIKERS

Germany had bigger stars than Miroslav Klose. But he always seemed to find the back of the net. He scored his 16th World Cup goal in 2014. It came in his fourth tournament. No men's player has more. However, another German, Gerd Müller, scored 14 goals in the 1970s. He played in only 13 games, compared to Klose's 24.

playing in the final. Then he added another in a 4–2 win. At 19, he was the youngest player to score in the final since Pelé. Mbappé played even better in 2022. He scored a tournament-high eight goals. And France almost repeated as champions. Mbappé even scored a hat trick in the final. But another superstar spoiled his performance.

Perhaps no player in soccer history had a better scoring touch than **Lionel Messi**. He played in his first World Cup in 2006 at age 18. In 2014, his play led Argentina to the final. But his team fell to a powerful German team. By 2022, there were doubts about Messi ever winning a World Cup. However, he put those doubts to rest. Among his seven goals in that tournament were two in the final. He also scored in the shootout. The performance secured Messi's legacy as one of the greatest players the sport has ever seen.

STAT SPOTLIGHT

WORLD CUP RECORD

CAREER MINUTES PLAYED

Lionel Messi: 2,314

AKERS
10

CHAPTER 3

THE WOMEN SHINE

The first Women's World Cup was held in 1991. **Michelle Akers** led the US attack. The center forward was big, strong, and intense. Akers scored 10 goals in the tournament. No player scored more. Akers recorded both of Team USA's goals in a 2–1 victory in the final.

By 1999, Akers's role had changed to midfielder. The Americans were loaded with talent. And they were playing in front of their home fans. The final came down to a shootout.

US goalie **Briana Scurry** made a diving save in the third round. And in the fifth round, defender **Brandi Chastain** scored the winning goal. This moment became one of the most famous in the history of women's sports.

German forward **Birgit Prinz** scored in her first World Cup start as a teenager in 1995. She went on to score 14 goals over five World Cups. At the time, no player had more. Prinz's scoring helped Germany win back-to-back championships in 2003 and 2007. That had

STAT SPOTLIGHT

WOMEN'S WORLD CUP RECORD

GOALS IN ONE GAME

Michelle Akers, United States: 5
(November 24, 1991)

Alex Morgan, United States: 5
(June 11, 2019)

never been done before. A strong defense also helped. In the 2007 tournament, Germany played six games. Goalie **Nadine Angerer** didn't allow a single goal.

Homare Sawa had played in four World Cups prior to 2011. Few had heard of the Japanese midfielder. However, she became

a household name in 2011. Her vision and determination lifted the squad. No matter what happened, Japan found a way to fight back. Sawa's clutch goals made Japan the first Asian team to win a World Cup.

By 2015, the United States hadn't won a championship in 16 years. **Carli Lloyd** helped end the drought. In the third minute of the final, the midfielder scored on a corner kick. She poked in a second goal two minutes later. Then, in the 16th minute, Lloyd ripped a shot from midfield. Japan's goalie was helpless as the ball flew over her head. A 5–2 victory put the Americans on top of the world again.

Megan Rapinoe helped win the 2015 championship. But the creative winger played even better in 2019. Rapinoe scored six goals and added three assists. Her variety of offensive skills helped the Americans win a fourth title. No team has won more.

MARVELOUS MARTA

In the early 2000s, women had to fight for opportunities to play soccer in Brazil. Marta did that, and then some. She became the world's best player. In 2007, her playmaking skills helped Brazil reach the final. Marta played in her sixth Women's World Cup in 2023. She never won a championship. But her 17 goals stood as the all-time scoring record.

TIMELINE

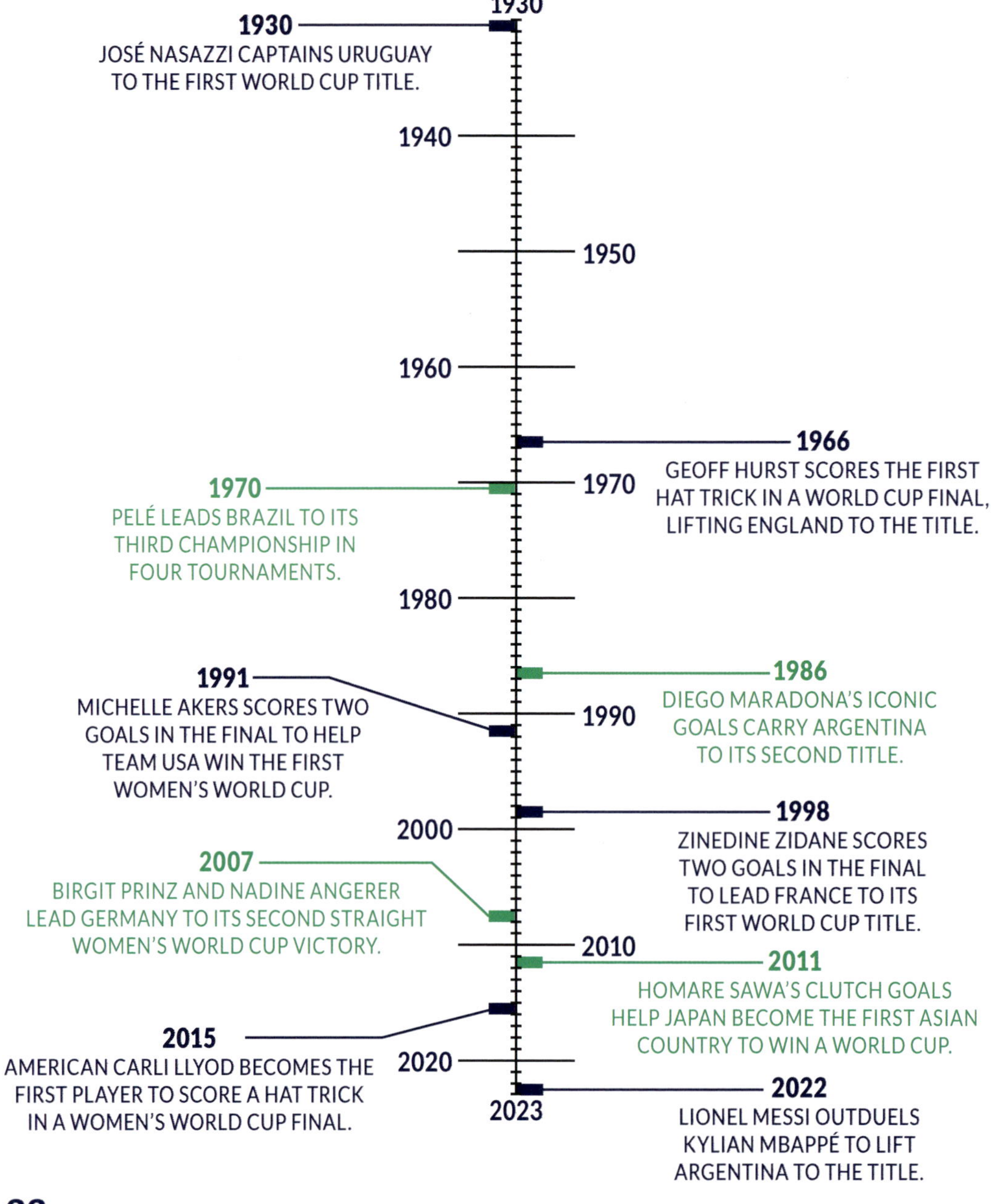

1930
JOSÉ NASAZZI CAPTAINS URUGUAY TO THE FIRST WORLD CUP TITLE.

1966
GEOFF HURST SCORES THE FIRST HAT TRICK IN A WORLD CUP FINAL, LIFTING ENGLAND TO THE TITLE.

1970
PELÉ LEADS BRAZIL TO ITS THIRD CHAMPIONSHIP IN FOUR TOURNAMENTS.

1986
DIEGO MARADONA'S ICONIC GOALS CARRY ARGENTINA TO ITS SECOND TITLE.

1991
MICHELLE AKERS SCORES TWO GOALS IN THE FINAL TO HELP TEAM USA WIN THE FIRST WOMEN'S WORLD CUP.

1998
ZINEDINE ZIDANE SCORES TWO GOALS IN THE FINAL TO LEAD FRANCE TO ITS FIRST WORLD CUP TITLE.

2007
BIRGIT PRINZ AND NADINE ANGERER LEAD GERMANY TO ITS SECOND STRAIGHT WOMEN'S WORLD CUP VICTORY.

2011
HOMARE SAWA'S CLUTCH GOALS HELP JAPAN BECOME THE FIRST ASIAN COUNTRY TO WIN A WORLD CUP.

2015
AMERICAN CARLI LLYOD BECOMES THE FIRST PLAYER TO SCORE A HAT TRICK IN A WOMEN'S WORLD CUP FINAL.

2022
LIONEL MESSI OUTDUELS KYLIAN MBAPPÉ TO LIFT ARGENTINA TO THE TITLE.

CHAMPIONSHIP FACTS

MEN'S WORLD CUP

First played: 1930

Most titles as a player: Pelé, 3

Most titles as a team: Brazil, 5

WOMEN'S WORLD CUP

First played: 1991

Most titles as a player: multiple players from Germany and the United States, 2

Most titles as a team: United States, 4

Stats are accurate through 2023.

MORE INFORMATION

To learn more about the World Cup, go to **pressboxbooks.com/AllAccess**.

These links are routinely monitored and updated to provide the most current information available.

GLOSSARY

captain
A player who serves as the leader of a team.

clutch
Having to do with a difficult situation when the outcome of the game is in question.

ethnic groups
Groups of people who share the same culture, language, or place of origin.

hat trick
When a player scores three or more goals in a game.

legacy
How a person or team is remembered.

modern
Relating to the recent past.

national teams
Sports teams made up only of players from a given country.

red card
A card the referee shows to a player who made a serious offense. The player must then leave the game.

shootout
When a tie game is decided by players taking penalty shots.

INDEX